On the LINE

My Story of Becoming the First African American Rockette

On the LINE

My Story of Becoming the First African American Rockette

Written by **Jennifer Jones** and **Lissette Norman**

Illustrated by **Robert Paul Jr.**

HARPER

An Imprint of HarperCollinsPublishers

What do you love doing most in the world?

    Well, I love to dance.

    I remember the moment dancing stole my heart. I was nine years old. On my first day of dance class, I discovered a new way to express my feelings, using every part of my body. I stretched my arms high above my head to let the world know: I'm here!

During ballet, I felt free
when I leaped through the air

and bold in jazz when
my feet went *tap, tap,*
tap across the floor.

That first day of dance class, I fell all the way in love with dancing!

But when I wasn't dancing, I was painfully shy. I was as quiet as a shut music box. And there was a reason I was so shy. My family was different from the other families in our town in New Jersey.

I can remember the first moment I realized how different we were. After dance class, my sister, my mom, and I went to the supermarket.

My mother let me keep on my tap shoes. I loved the sound my tapping feet made on the store's linoleum floor. It was like an invitation to dance.

As my mom pushed our cart through the store, I did my favorite tap step—with my hands on my hips, I back-flapped my way down the aisles far ahead of her.

Suddenly a frowning store clerk stopped me. "What do you think you're doing?"

"Pr-practicing a step I learned in dance class," I said in a voice so small, I was surprised she heard me.

"Girls like you don't become dancers," the woman said. Then she yelled out: "Whose child is this?"

"She's mine!" my mother said, rushing up to us. Her face was mixed with worry and relief.

"She doesn't look like she's yours," the store clerk said.

The woman didn't believe her because my mom is white and my skin is a beautiful golden brown. My sister and I were among the first "brown" babies to come from interracial marriages, which were illegal in parts of the United States until 1967.

My dad is Black, and back then, many white people didn't think people of different races should marry. But my mom wouldn't stand for the woman's ignorance.

"You don't know what you're talking about," she replied.

SALE
2 For 1

When we got home from grocery shopping, my mother called my dad at work—not to tell him about the woman at the supermarket. Instead, she asked him to bring home a large piece of linoleum.

My sister, Cheryl,
and I helped him bring
it into the house.

He took the piece of linoleum down to the basement and laid it flat on the cement floor. Then my mother told me: "Dance the way you danced in the grocery store, my sweet child."

And I did. Every day, while my dad sat at his desk to work, I danced.

While Black people marched in the streets for equal rights, I danced.

I tapped and twirled on my sweet-sounding piece of linoleum.

It didn't matter that my family was different. Dancing freed me from the fear of my family not looking like anyone else's and people who didn't agree with interracial marriage. Dancing made me feel less alone.

For my fourth-grade recital, I danced in front of a large audience for the first time. As I tapped and twirled, it was like the entire auditorium moved with me. I forgot about my fears, and being so brave was a little like magic.

The stage felt like home. And I discovered I loved myself most when I was dancing.

I heard the loud cheers and applause at the end, and I was sure I would dance forever. But the store clerk's voice still echoed in my head. And the spotlight on me faded.

"Can girls my color become dancers?" I asked my mother that night. My mom's face lit up.

"Yes, and I'm going to show you that girls your color can be anything they dream of."

Soon after, my parents took my sister and me to see *The Wiz* on Broadway. I watched, mesmerized by the all-Black cast. My parents had planted a seed inside me: I can be Black and dance on a grand stage too.

When I was nineteen, I auditioned for the Radio City Rockettes. For me, becoming a Rockette meant I would be a trailblazer, not only for me, but for other dancers who looked like me. Since the dance company started performing in 1925, there had never been a Black Rockette. Believing I could be on the line required lots of absolutely-very-possibly kind of imagination.

I didn't see another Black dancer on the long, long audition line and considered leaving a few times. Then my mother's tender voice spoke in my head:
Girls your color can be anything they dream of.

It felt like a million eyes were on me when they checked my height with the official Rockettes measuring stick. If I didn't make the height, I'd be turned away.

And not bringing the proper shoes sure didn't help. But no matter. I was ready to show off my skills in ballet, tap, and jazz.

First, a wave of
violin strings sent me
pirouette-spiraling.

Then snappy rhythms
got me toe-tapping and
jazz-jamming all about.

Hardest of all were the twenty eye-level kicks. Standing tall and straight-backed, I kicked as high as my legs could go.

Not nervous but buzzing with excitement, I danced like I had done the routines a hundred times before.

I danced like I belonged.

"She's talking about me!" I yelled when I heard it on the news a few months later.

"I always knew you could do it!" my mother said with pride piled high in her heart.

1st African American Rockette

I never set out to break racial barriers, but I was ready to take on my new role. And if I hadn't stayed on that audition line, I would've never made it onto the Rockettes line. Stepping onto the Radio City Music Hall stage for the first time took my breath away. My stomach was a carnival of butterflies. Many people came to see the first African American Rockette.

To calm my nerves, I imagined I was down in our basement, dancing on a piece of sweet-sounding linoleum with just my parents and sister there, cheering me on.

Thirty-six Rockettes dressed in identical, colorful costumes. A microphone hidden in the heels of our tap shoes. Seventy-two unified legs performing three hundred eye-high kicks. We all danced as one.

Afterward, I cried with joy. Doing what I loved most had led me to one of the grandest stages in the world. That day, I made history as the first African American Rockette.

When the
show was over, I exited from
the Radio City Music Hall stage door.
My family stood in a crowd of people waiting to get my
autograph. There were also news reporters requesting interviews
and photographers with bright flashing lights. I reached out for my mother's
hand and pulled her into a tight hug.

She stood beside me, and together we posed for pictures. Her endless support
and belief in me helped the seed she planted in me long before blossom into that
sweet historic day.

There are many stories like mine all around us.

Stories of people who found the thing they love doing the most and never let go of that love.

Stories about families and communities that help us discover where we belong.

What will your story be?

The world can't wait to find out!

More about **Jennifer Jones**
and the **ROCKETTES**

JENNIFER JONES was born and
raised in New Jersey. She began dancing
at age six, mastering tap, ballet, jazz, and
modern dance.

In 1987, at the age of nineteen, she
became the first African American
Rockette. In doing so, she also changed
the longstanding Radio City Music Hall
policy against hiring African Americans
for its Rockettes' chorus line so as not to
distract from its hallmark rigid skin color uniformity. She had to fight to
get tights that matched her skin tone. Afterward, every Rockette initiate got a pair of
tights that matched perfectly to their skin tone without having to ask.

Her first performance as a Rockette was in 1988 during the Super Bowl XXII
halftime show, "Something Grand."

She was a Rockette for fifteen years.

Jennifer continued to transcend racial barriers by becoming the first African
American woman to be crowned Miss Morris County Pageant Queen in her native New
Jersey in 1989.

In 2001, Jennifer went on to perform in the Broadway show *42nd Street*, the same
year it won the Tony Award for Best Revival of a Musical.

Along with this book, she's designed a Dancing Jenn doll. The doll serves as a
reminder to children that thoughts become things and to live their dreams out loud.

Acknowledgments

Gratitude to my ancestors, upon whose shoulders I stand.

Thank you to my incredible and ingenious agent, Johanna, for encouraging me to write a children's book. Without you and your expertise, this would have happened much later. Much appreciation and gratitude to the entire HarperCollins publishing team, who believed in my story. Claudia, Alyson, and Karina, I am forever grateful for your fiery passion and your loyal guidance and support.

Lissette, thank you for helping me tell my story so gracefully, magically, and poetically. Robert, master illustrator, thank you for bringing color, brightness, and life to the words.

To my sisters, Cheryl and Peaches, who are the epitome of sisterhood, thank you for always being there for me and us for each other. From our deep belly laughs to our ugliest cries.

To Mom and Dad, Linda and Booker, thank you for all the dance classes, the linoleum floor in the basement, and taking me to see *The Wiz* on Broadway time after time. I am forever grateful for knowing what a backstage door is.

My children, Zachary and Isabella, you are my heart. My love for you is unconditional.

And last, to my charismatic and sarcastic husband, Jeffrey, who has given me his love and humor throughout the years."

To my children, Zachary and Isabella. Dream big,
believe in yourself, and live your life out loud.
And to all the Black dancers who came before me—
I stand on your shoulders.
—J.J.

Dancing is an art form and without variety, there is
no rhythm. I dedicate this to every dancer of color.
—R.P.

On the Line: My Story of Becoming the First African American Rockette

Text copyright © 2023 by Jennifer Jones

Illustrations copyright © 2023 by Robert Paul Jr.

All rights reserved. Manufactured in Italy.

Library of Congress Control Number: 2023934377

ISBN 978-0-06-308706-4

The artist used Autodesk Sketchbook Pro to create the digital illustrations for this book.

Typography by Rachel Zegar

23 24 25 26 27 RTLO 10 9 8 7 6 5 4 3 2 1

First Edition